THE ENCYCLOPEDIA
OF
awesome
DINOSAURS

© Aladdin Books Ltd 2000
Produced by
Aladdin Books Ltd
28 Percy Street
London W1P 0LD

ISBN 0-7613-0846-6

First published in the United States in 2000 by
Copper Beech Books,
an imprint of
The Millbrook Press
2 Old New Milford Road
Brookfield, Connecticut 06804

Editor:
Kathy Gemmell

Designers:
Flick, Book Design and Graphics
Simon Morse

Illustrators:
James Field, Ross Watton—SGA
Additional illustrations: Sarah Smith—SGA
Cartoons: Jo Moore
Certain illustrations have appeared in earlier
books created by Aladdin Books.

Printed in Belgium
All rights reserved

Cataloging-in-Publication data is on file
at the Library of Congress

THE
ENCYCLOPEDIA
OF
awesome
DINOSAURS

Michael Benton

COPPER BEECH BOOKS
Brookfield · Connecticut

Contents

Introduction

Discover for yourself the most amazing things about these creatures that roamed Earth millions and millions of years ago. What did they eat? How did they live? Where did they go? What new discoveries are scientists making? Chapter by chapter, this book gives you the latest information about fearsome meat eaters, giant lumbering plant eaters, duck lookalikes, and spiky armored dinosaurs. Learn about fossils—where they are found and who looks for them— and find out how you can name a dinosaur after yourself!

Spot and count!

? Q: Why watch out for these boxes?

A: They give answers to the dinosaur questions you always wanted to ask.

zoom in on...

Dinosaur bits

Look out for these boxes to take a closer look at dinosaur features.

Awesome facts
Watch out for these diamonds to learn more about the truly weird and wonderful facts about dinosaurs and their world.

Chapter 1
The world of dinosaurs

Dinosaurs were among the most successful animals of all time. They lived on Earth for over 160 million years, and they were big. Some were very big indeed. Scientists called paleontologists study remains that have been preserved in ancient rocks. They have unearthed amazing information and are constantly making exciting new discoveries.

This insect has been preserved in amber.

Archelon

Carnotaurus

Euoplocephalus

Awesome facts

In the film *Jurassic Park*, scientists used bits of DNA (genes) preserved in fossils to bring dinosaurs back to life. We know, however, that this is impossible.

6

Pteranodon

Tarbosaurus

Lambeosaurus

Baryonyx

Q: What are dinosaur remains called?

A: The bones, shells, leaves, and other remains that have been preserved in rock are called fossils. Fossils of dinosaurs and of plants and animals that lived with them have been found all over the world.

Albertosaurus

Styracosaurus

MESOZOIC ERA: 250–65 MILLION YEARS AGO (MYA)
The Mesozoic era, when the dinosaurs lived, is split into three periods.

Triassic period
Dinosaurs appeared halfway through this time.

Jurassic period
Age of giant dinosaurs and first birds

Cretaceous period
A time of success for dinosaurs. Their last phase.

Fish, amphibians, and early reptiles appeared before the Mesozoic era.

250 mya

205 mya

145 mya

65 mya

Today

When they lived

The dinosaurs lived between 230 and 65 million years ago (mya). This is a very long time, and it was a very long time ago. It's hard enough to imagine hundreds of years ago, let alone millions. Scientists know when dinosaurs lived because they can date the rocks in which their fossils are found. They do this by studying the radioactivity of the rocks, then classing them on a scale called the geological time scale. This is split into sections called eras.

8

At the start of the age of the dinosaurs, the continents were all joined together as one great supercontinent called Pangaea. Over millions of years, the Atlantic Ocean opened up and Pangaea split apart. The continents drifted (moved slowly) to their present positions. They are still moving a few hundredths of an inch each year.

Today

50 mya

100 mya

Pangaea

200 mya

Continental drift

Q: Why is the dinosaur age split into sections?

A: The Mesozoic era—the time on the geological scale when dinosaurs lived—is split into periods, based on the rocks and creatures around at the time. The Triassic came first. Its name comes from the Latin for three, *tri*, because the period had three distinct parts. Many fossils from this time have been found in Germany. The Jurassic is named after the Jura mountains in France, where rocks of this age are common. Cretaceous comes from the Greek for chalk, *creta*, a common rock from this period.

Triassic period: 250–205 mya

Jurassic period: 205–145 mya

Cretaceous period: 145–65 mya

9

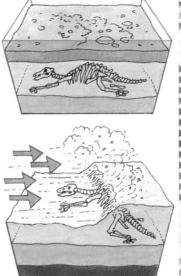

Q: How did a dinosaur become a fossil?

A: Small meat-eating animals ate the flesh from the dead dinosaur's bones. Some bones rotted. Others were buried under layers of sand or mud. These turned into fossils over time, as tiny spaces in the bones filled with rock. Millions of years later, the fossilized bones are uncovered by water or wind action.

To protect fossilized dinosaur bones, strips of cloth are soaked in plaster and water, then wrapped around the bone in layers. As the plaster dries, it forms a tough protective shell.

Digging them up

Digging dinosaurs is a long and difficult business. First, you have to find a skeleton, then get it out of the rock and bring it home. Then begins the slow process of cleaning it, making sure it doesn't crumble into bits.

Paleontologists (fossil experts) make maps and take photographs at the dig site, so that they can tell later exactly where everything was found.

Sometimes, dinosaur fossils can surprise scientists. In 2000, an amazing specimen of the dinosaur *Thescelosaurus* was found in South Dakota, with its heart preserved. This seems incredible. Normally only the bones survive, but this dinosaur carcass must have been buried in dry sand before it began to rot. So even some flesh was preserved.

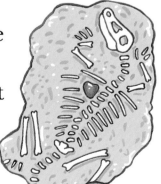

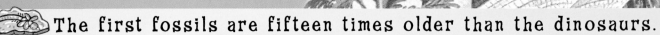

Awesome facts

In the swamp forests of 320 mya, there were dragonflies as big as seagulls. Dragonflies live on today, but none is as big as this prehistoric monster.

Hylonomus

Chapter 2
Dinosaur evolution

Dinosaurs were not the first prehistoric creatures on Earth. The oldest fossils—very simple microbes—date back to an amazing 3,500 million years ago (mya). The first sea animals appeared 600 mya, the first fish 500 mya, and the first reptiles 320 mya. The dinosaurs, also reptiles, evolved (developed) from these early reptiles. The first dinosaurs were found in rocks 230 million years old.

Up to 400 mya, there was not much life on land—just some small plants and bugs. Then some unusual fish that could breathe with lungs as well as gills began to live on land for short periods. By 370 mya, one of these air-breathing fish had evolved legs. This was the first amphibian. Like modern frogs, these first amphibians still had to lay their eggs in water.

The first reptile survived on a diet of cockroaches, scorpions, and centipedes (above). It was called *Hylonomus,* and lived in the great swamp forests of Canada 320 mya.

13

Dinosaur groups

There were five main groups of dinosaurs: the meat eaters, called theropods; the big, long-necked plant eaters, called sauropodomorphs; the armored plant eaters, called thyreophorans; the horned dinosaurs, called marginocephalians; and the two-legged plant eaters, called ornithopods.

Carnotaurus
(Saurischia)

Hypsilophodon
(Ornithischia)

SAURISCHIA

THEROPODA	SAUROPODOMORPHA

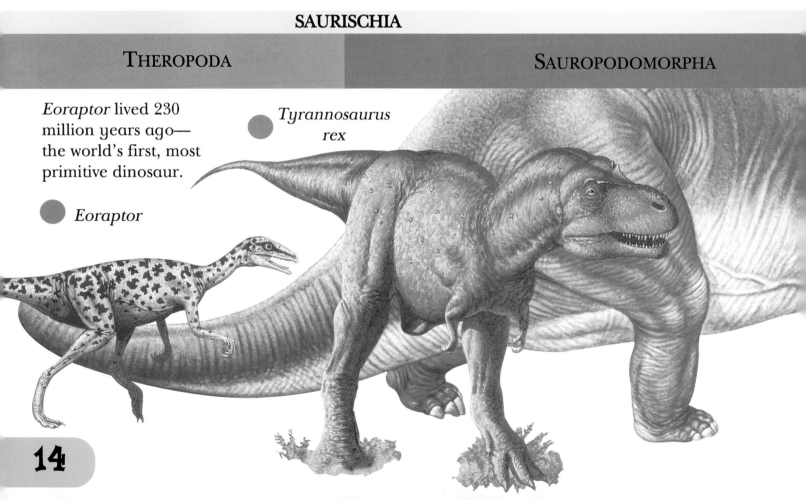

Eoraptor lived 230 million years ago— the world's first, most primitive dinosaur.

● *Eoraptor*

● *Tyrannosaurus rex*

14

All dinosaurs are classed into one of two subgroups, called the Saurischia and the Ornithischia, according to the arrangement of their three hip bones (left). The Saurischia, or "lizard hipped," had the three hip bones all pointing in different directions. The Ornithischia, or "bird hipped," had both of the lower hip bones running backward.

Q: Are there any dinosaurs left?

A: The monster dinosaurs all died out long ago, but birds are living dinosaurs. *Archaeopteryx*, the first bird, lived 150 million years ago. It is the link between dinosaurs and modern birds, with wings and feathers (like a bird), but also teeth in its jaws, sharp claws on its hands, and a long, bony tail.

● *Apatosaurus*

ORNITHISCHIA

| THYREOPHORA | MARGINOCEPHALIA | ORNITHOPODA |

● *Einosaurus*

Corythosaurus

● *Stegosaurus*

15

Tyrannosaurus rex

Big meat eaters like *T. rex* ate the larger plant eaters. *T. rex* probably wasn't very fast or very bright. It didn't need to be. It was so big it could attack almost any other dinosaur.

Troodon

T. rex used its massive teeth to tear strips from its prey's flesh.

Chapter 3
Meat eaters

Meat-eating dinosaurs, called the theropods, ranged from turkey-sized dinosaurs to the awesome *Tyrannosaurus rex*. Theropods of different sizes ate prey of different sizes. This meant that several species could live side by side.

Ornithomimus

What is T. rex eating?

In the Late Cretaceous of Canada, smaller meat eaters lived alongside the huge *T. rex*. *Troodon* hunted lizards, mammals, and even insects. It relied on speed and intelligence. *Ornithomimus* ate small plant-eating dinosaurs and the young of larger ones.

What makes a meat eater?

All meat eaters had sharp claws. They also had sharp, curved teeth pointing backward that pushed any struggling prey farther into the gaping jaws. One of the most fearsome meat eaters was *Deinonychus.*

Deinonychus

 Q: How did *Deinonychus* use its toe claw?

A: It had one huge claw on each foot, on the second toe. When running, it held the claw off the ground so it would not become blunt. But when it attacked, it raised its foot and slashed downward with the claw, as shown here.

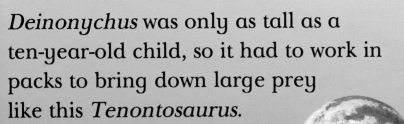

Deinonychus was only as tall as a ten-year-old child, so it had to work in packs to bring down large prey like this *Tenontosaurus*.

Tenontosaurus

Balancing

Two-legged dinosaurs, like *Deinonychus* and the other meat eaters, were like seesaws, balanced over their back legs. The front of the body had to weigh the same as the tail, or the dinosaur would fall on its nose. It had to hold its backbone flat when it ran and flick its massive tail around to keep its balance.

zoom in on...

Awesome factS

Most dinosaurs were pretty stupid, but *Deinonychus* had a big brain. It needed it, in order to balance, see well, and be able to communicate with the rest of the pack.

19

Smash and grab

One of the first meat-eating dinosaurs was *Herrerasaurus*, from the Late Triassic of Argentina, 230 million years ago. Medium-sized and good at hunting, *Herrerasaurus* ate mammal-like reptiles called cynodonts, which lived in burrows.

Herrerasaurus

Herrerasaurus had the advantage in a sudden attack. It could creep up silently, dart its head into a cynodont burrow, and race off with a cub before the parent could do anything.

Q: How did dinosaur jaws open so wide?

A: Most meat eaters had very narrow skulls. There wasn't much in there except teeth and jaw muscles—the brain was pretty tiny. But when a meat eater opened its jaws, its whole mouth stretched sideways to take a bigger bite.

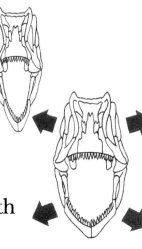

The ancestors of mammals belonged to the same mammal-like reptile group as cynodonts. Some cynodonts probably had hair and were warm-blooded. They could hunt at night, unlike the cold-blooded early dinosaurs.

Meat eaters had powerful hands. Early ones, like *Herrerasaurus*, had four or five muscular fingers, each with a long, sharp claw. Most later meat eaters had only three fingers, and some, like *T. rex*, had only two.

Cynodont

zoom in on...

Predator numbers

Meat eaters were much rarer than plant eaters. This is because there must always be far fewer predators than prey animals, like lions and antelope today.

21

Hunt to the death

Fossilized footprints show that meat-eating dinosaurs walked and swam in lakes. The eighteen-foot-long *Ceratosaurus* was the terror of North America 150 million years ago. But it took more than one to bring down *Apatosaurus*, a huge but slow-moving plant eater.

Awesome facts

Ceratosaurus had horns on its head, in front of the eyes. These made it look more frightening and may have been used for fighting.

Ceratosaurus

 Q: Why did meat eater skulls have so many holes?

A: Holes are lighter than bones, and a light skull can move faster. So a meat eater had thin bones with very big holes between them for its ears, eyes, nostrils, and jaw muscles.

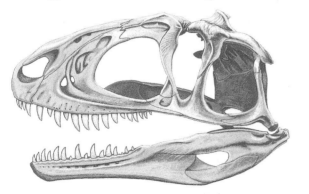

Small and medium-sized meat eaters like *Ceratosaurus* could run fast. They moved at twelve to eighteen miles per hour, which is about the fastest you could sprint over a short distance. Bigger meat eaters like *Albertosaurus* may not have been able to move as fast because they were so much heavier.

Albertosaurus

Apatosaurus

Pack hunting was a risky business. Although *Apatosaurus* did not have powerful teeth or sharp claws, it could whack out with its powerful tail and stun a predator. But if the *Ceratosaurus* kept biting into its flesh, the *Apatosaurus* would eventually become weak and die.

What's in a name?

Dinosaur means "terrible lizard." Although we now know that they were not lizards, dinosaur names often tell us something about them. Named in 1884, savage meat eater *Ceratosaurus* means "horned lizard," referring to the horns on its face.

Megalosaurus "big lizard"

Dilophosaurus "two-ridged lizard"

The fierce meat eater *Yangchuanosaurus*, from an area of China called Yangchuan, attacks a Chinese plant eater.

Yangchuanosaurus "Yangchuan lizard"

Archaeopteryx "ancient wing"

Q: Who gives dinosaurs their names?

A: Dinosaurs are named by their discoverers. About twenty new species are still being named every year. If you find a new dinosaur skeleton, which has never been named, you can make up a name and publish it!

Megalosaurus, named in 1824, means "big lizard." This drawing shows what scientists then thought it looked like.

Richard Owen made up the word "dinosaur" in 1842.

Othniel Marsh (left) and Edward Cope (right) named more dinosaurs than anyone else between 1870 and 1900, including *Ceratosaurus*, *Allosaurus*, and *Stegosaurus*.

Ceratosaurus "horned lizard"

zoom in on...

Skull horns

Allosaurus, like most meat eaters, had knobs and lumps on its skull. What were they for? Maybe they just made its face look more scary. When male dinosaurs squared up to each other, *Allosaurus*, with its loud growl and its bumps, would usually have been the winner.

Allosaurus

How many flies can you count?

All over the world

Meat eaters lived all over the world. *Allosaurus*, for example, is best known from the Late Jurassic of North America, 150 million years ago, but remains have also been found in Tanzania in Africa and possibly even in Australia.

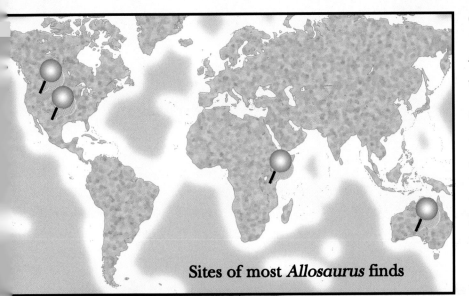

Sites of most *Allosaurus* finds

The worldwide spread of *Allosaurus* is not surprising when you remember that the continents were joined together as the supercontinent Pangaea in the Jurassic (see page 9). *Allosaurus* could have wandered from one end of the world to the other.

Awesome facts

The Australian *Allosaurus* find is not confirmed. It is in Early Cretaceous rocks, 50 million years younger than the other finds, and is only of part of a leg.

Tiny and terrible

Some meat eaters were so tiny that a big plant-eating dinosaur like *Apatosaurus* would not even see them. But these midgets were pretty scary if you were a ratlike mammal or a lizard. Small size went with intelligence and speed.

Compsognathus lived in what is now Germany, and was the smallest dinosaur— a mere twenty-three inches long from its snout to the tip of its tail. An amazing fossil of this tiny hunter (right) even shows its last meal—a complete skeleton of the lizard *Bavarisaurus*, inside its rib cage.

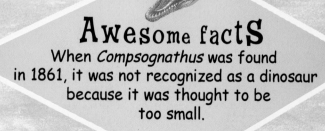

Awesome facts
When *Compsognathus* was found in 1861, it was not recognized as a dinosaur because it was thought to be too small.

A small flock of *Compsognathus* are scattered (right) by a giant plant eater. These little dinosaurs could move fast. They may even have had a fine covering of feathers over their bodies. They fed on lizards, frogs, and dragonflies.

Q: Were some dinosaurs really as small as chickens?

A: If the fully adult *Compsognathus* was only twenty-three inches long, its babies must have been tiny. Scientists know about quite a number of dinosaur young, and many of them were the size of a chicken, or even smaller.

Compsognathus

Feathers are made from keratin, the same horny protein that makes up your nails and your hair. Feathers are not often preserved as fossils because they normally rot before the carcass is buried. However, in some cases, if the feather is buried quickly, it can survive as a fossil.

Sinosauropteryx

Feathered find

Until the 1990s, feathered dinosaurs were only a wild theory. Then some startling finds in China proved that many small meat eaters had them. *Sinosauropteryx* is one of the newly discovered Chinese feathered dinosaurs, and is thought to be a relative of *Compsognathus*.

Compsognathus and *Archaeopteryx,* the first bird, were found in the same rocks in southern Germany. Both were named in 1861. Paleontologists soon noticed that their skeletons were very similar, and they suggested that dinosaurs had given rise to birds. This has been debated hotly for years, but it now seems clear that birds really are living theropod dinosaurs.

Archaeopteryx

Compsognathus

zoom in on...

Wings

A wing is just a fairly long arm that has feathers on it. *Deinonychus* had long arms with strong hands, probably covered with short feathers. It is not hard to see how this could have evolved into a flying wing if the feathers grew longer.

Deinonychus

Fishing claws

Most meat eaters ate other dinosaurs or smaller land animals. One group, the spinosaurids, had crocodile-shaped skulls and may have been fish eaters. Perhaps they used their strong hands to swipe fish out of the water, just as bears do today.

Awesome facts

The spinosaurid *Baryonyx* from southern England was found by accident in 1983 by William Walker as he walked through his local brickyard.

Baryonyx

Q: Why did spinosaurids have crocodile skulls?

A: The long, low snout and numerous teeth of the spinosaurids must have been ideal for holding struggling fish. Stronger jaws are needed only for larger prey. Spinosaurids looked far more like modern crocodiles than like other meat eaters.

Crocodile

Some spinosaurids had long spines on their vertebrae (backbone). These may have had a thin covering of skin—a kind of sail—running along them. Perhaps this was used to control body temperature—to take in heat when the body was cold and to give it off when the body was overheated.

The spinosaurid *Baryonyx*, from the Early Cretaceous of southern England, crouched silently beside a river and swiped out fish with its long-clawed hand.

Oviraptor means "egg thief." It was named in 1924, and has had a bad reputation ever since. Paleontologists then thought that this toothless theropod fed on eggs. But the reason it was found close to nests containing eggs was that it was a good parent, caring for its own young!

Oviraptor

How many eggs can you count?

zoom in on...

Dinosaur eggs

Scientists dissect dinosaur eggs, and sometimes they find tiny bones inside. This tiny embryo lay curled up inside the eggshell—it must have died before it could hatch.

Oviraptor embryo

As good parents, dinosaurs probably helped to protect their young after they had hatched. They may have brought back food, partly chewed, to feed to their young. Disgusting maybe, but that's what many birds do.

Nesting

An astonishing find in 1995 in Mongolia showed that some meat eaters sat on their eggs, just like modern birds, to protect them and keep them warm (or cool). Most modern reptiles lay their eggs then leave them.

Q: How big was a *T. rex* tooth?

A: *T. rex* had teeth the size of steak knives. The tooth had two halves. The upper crown, which did the cutting, was the size of a banana. The root, hidden in the jawbone, was just as big.

T. rex—terrifying hunter or humble scavenger? Some paleontologists think that *T. rex* was so massive that it could not have moved fast. It might have lumbered about slowly, looking for rotting carcasses that had been killed by smaller, swifter meat eaters.

Sizing up

The meat-eating dinosaur *Tyrannosaurus rex*, from the Late Cretaceous of North America, was a monster. At thirty-nine feet long and weighing up to nearly nine tons, *T. rex* was truly awesome: It could swallow you in one gulp. But was it the biggest?

T. rex footprint

Other huge dinosaurs, such as *Carcharodontosaurus* from North Africa and *Giganotosaurus* from Argentina, may have been longer than *T. rex*, but they were not as heavy.

Tyrannosaurus rex

zoom in on...

Poop!

In 1998, Canadian scientists found a giant dinosaur poop, about three feet long, containing dinosaur bones. Whodunnit? *T. rex*, most probably.

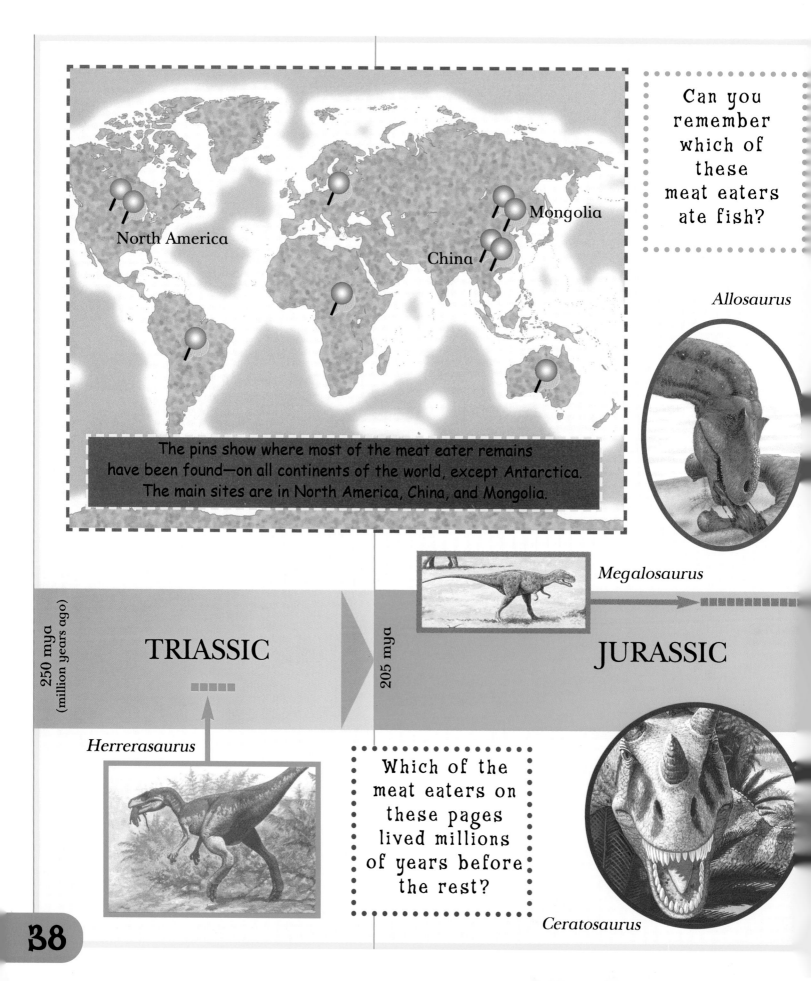

Mongolia

North America

China

The pins show where most of the meat eater remains have been found—on all continents of the world, except Antarctica. The main sites are in North America, China, and Mongolia.

Can you remember which of these meat eaters ate fish?

Allosaurus

Megalosaurus

250 mya (million years ago)

205 mya

TRIASSIC

JURASSIC

Herrerasaurus

Which of the meat eaters on these pages lived millions of years before the rest?

Ceratosaurus

Meat eaters' world

From the tiny *Compsognathus* to the awesome *T. rex*, theropods were the terrors of the Mesozoic era. They are known from all corners of the world and existed for 165 million years.

T. rex

Sinosauropteryx

Albertosaurus

Oviraptor

Baryonyx

145 mya

CRETACEOUS

65 mya

Compsognathus

Deinonychus

Ornithomimus

Troodon

39

Chapter 4
Giant plant eaters

Which sauropod is reaching the highest?

The dinosaur group called the sauropodomorphs included the sauropods, which were the huge, long-necked plant eaters like *Apatosaurus* and *Diplodocus*, and the earlier, smaller prosauropods, such as *Plateosaurus*.

Apatosaurus

The most famous giant plant eaters
lived in the Late Jurassic, 150 million
years ago, of North America.
Diplodocus and *Apatosaurus* fed
on low plants, while *Brachiosaurus*,
with its hugely long neck, could
reach up into the treetops.

Brachiosaurus

Diplodocus

Awesome factS

The bigger kinds of sauropods
weighed around fifty-five tons. But the very
biggest individuals might have
weighed even more
than this.

The giant plant eaters were generally much, much bigger than the meat eaters that lived beside them. A typical meat eater such as *Allosaurus* only weighed two or three tons (an elephant weighs four or five tons). Most of the sauropods weighed at least ten or twenty times as much.

zoom in on...

Biting bits

Sauropod teeth were often shaped like pegs or pencils. Some, like *Diplodocus*, only had teeth at the front of the jaws. These were used only for biting off plants. Sauropods did not chew food before swallowing.

Diplodocus

Camarasaurus had a shorter neck and tail than many of the giant plant eaters. At sixty-five feet long and weighing perhaps twenty-two tons, it was also smaller. *Camarasaurus* had particularly strong teeth for a sauropod—perhaps this was because it ate tougher plant food than the others.

Camarasaurus

Awesome factS

One *Camarasaurus* skeleton clearly shows deep tooth marks on its bones. These probably came from the fearsome flesh eater *Allosaurus*.

Pegs for teeth

Despite their massive size, the sauropods had pretty weak teeth. It's hard to imagine how these enormous plant eaters managed to break off enough leaves and twigs to survive. Most of them probably never stopped eating.

Ancestors

The giant sauropods' ancestors were much smaller. An early sauropodomorph was *Thecodontosaurus*, a two-legged, six foot-long animal from the Late Triassic of southern England.

Thecodontosaurus

How many fingers do they have?

44

Q: Why are they called sauropodomorphs?

A: "Sauropodomorph" is a bit of a mouthful, meaning "lizard feet forms." The name is not ideal, since their feet are more like elephants' feet than lizards' feet. But the name sticks.

The bones of *Thecodontosaurus* were found in 1836 in broken limestone and sandstone from a cave. The animals must have fallen in by accident.

In the cave deposits (above), skeletons of male and female *Thecodontosaurus* adults, as well as the skeleton of a baby, have been found. *Thecodontosaurus* had to look after their young carefully, as there were many big meat eaters around in the Late Triassic.

45

Plateosaurus had a long, narrow skull. It could open its mouth wide, and used its muscular tongue to grasp leaves. Its small teeth could only cut soft plants.

Awesome facts

At one site in Germany, forty individual *Plateosaurus* were found. They had all been swept away in a torrent and were killed together.

zoom in on...

Hands

Plateosaurus had five strong fingers. Its thumb was broad and very muscular and had a deep claw on it. It used its hands to rake leaves together before stuffing them into its mouth.

Thumb claw

Feeding

One of the first giant plant eaters was the prosauropod *Plateosaurus* from the Late Triassic of Germany. It used its strong hands and powerful tongue to find the huge amounts of food it needed to survive.

Unusual polished stones have been found inside the rib cages of many dinosaurs. These were probably stomach stones, or gastroliths. Dinosaurs could not chew their food. So they swallowed pebbles, which sat in the stomach and helped to grind up the unchewed food. Modern hens do this by swallowing grit.

How many *Plateosaurus* can you count?

Melanorosaurus, a large prosauropod from the Early Jurassic of South Africa, was a close relative of *Riojasaurus*. This giant prosauropod is known only from incomplete remains.

Melanorosaurus

Riojasaurus had a huge size advantage over meat-eating dinosaurs. However, small meat eaters may have hunted in packs, perhaps separating young animals from the herd and attacking them.

Where in the world?

By the end of the Triassic, some prosauropods had become huge. *Riojasaurus* from Argentina was thirty-three feet long. It most likely walked on all fours most of the time, but maybe went up on its hind legs to feed in trees.

Riojasaurus

Coelophysis

In the Late Triassic and Early Jurassic, the Atlantic Ocean had not yet begun to open up. This meant that *Riojasaurus* and *Melanorosaurus* could easily walk between what is now South America and South Africa. The land connection existed for another fifty million years.

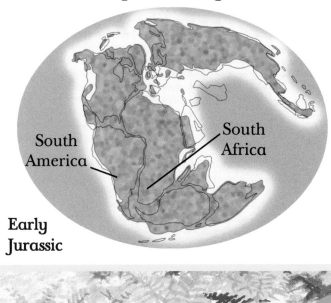

South Africa

South America

Early Jurassic

Riojasaurus could kill small meat eaters with one whack of its powerful tail. It could also defend itself by swiping at them with its hands or feet. Its claws were designed for gathering plant food, but they could also deliver a vicious cut.

The most complete *Cetiosaurus* was found in 1980 in eastern England. The skeleton was carefully excavated and taken to a museum in Leicester, where it is now on display. Paleontologists need to take great care when they excavate bones, as the bones can easily break or get mixed up.

Awesome facts

Cetiosaurus means "whale lizard." It was named in 1841 by Sir Richard Owen, who only had a few bones to study and thought it was a giant crocodile.

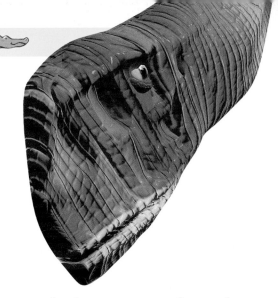

Skeletons

By the Middle Jurassic, 175 million years ago, the prosauropods had gone and the sauropods ruled Earth. One of the first to be found was *Cetiosaurus*, a medium-sized sauropod from England, which measured about thirty feet long.

As more skeletons are found, scientists can construct more and more accurate computer models of dinosaurs. These can be animated to show how different dinosaurs moved.

zoom in on...

Cetiosaurus skeleton

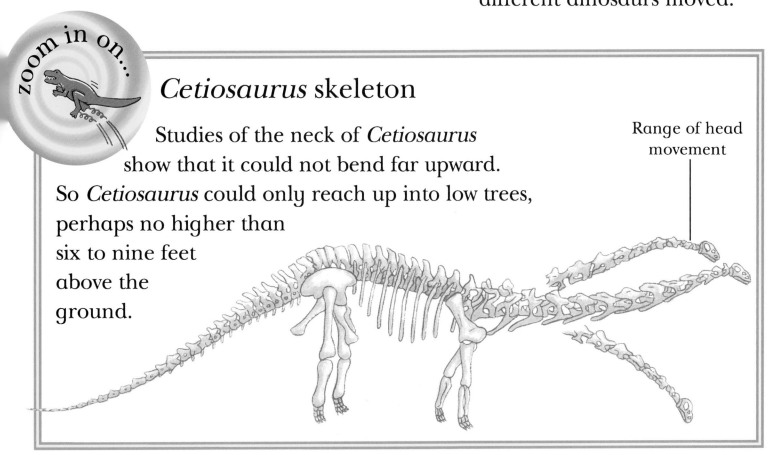

Studies of the neck of *Cetiosaurus* show that it could not bend far upward. So *Cetiosaurus* could only reach up into low trees, perhaps no higher than six to nine feet above the ground.

Range of head movement

zoom in on...

Medicine

Dinosaur bones were used as a kind of medicine in China. Doctors ground up these "dragon bones" to make pills with magic properties.

Long neck

Sauropods all had long necks, but *Mamenchisaurus* from the Late Jurassic of China takes the prize. Its neck was thirty-three feet long, nearly half its total body length of seventy-two. This might be the longest neck that ever existed on Earth!

Mamenchisaurus

Q: How did a sauropod's neck stay up?

Diplodocus

Muscles

A: There were huge muscles running along the neck, some of them like the cables on a crane. By pulling on the muscles along the top of the neck, a sauropod could lift its neck up and down. This took a lot of energy, so most sauropods probably kept their heads down as much as possible.

Sauropods used their long necks to reach for food. This means that they did not have to move their massive body when they spotted a tasty bunch of leaves—they just reached out with their neck.

What kind of plant are they eating?

Huge and heavy

The heaviest sauropod may have been *Brachiosaurus*, known from the Late Jurassic of North America and Tanzania in Africa. This monster was seventy-five feet long and weighed as much as fifty or even seventy tons. It is most famous, however, for its astonishing height.

Brachiosaurus

 Q: How did *Brachiosaurus* support its weight?

A: The skeleton of a sauropod was like a huge bridge. The legs held up the weight and the backbone had high spines over the shoulder and hips. Strong muscles spanned the backbone to balance the long neck and tail.

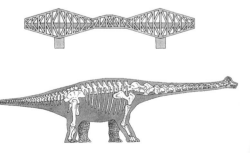

As animals get bigger, their legs get fatter. This is because the legs have to support the increasing weight. Camels have thin legs, elephants have legs like pillars, and sauropods had legs like huge treetrunks.

Awesome factS

Scientists have calculated that, in order to support their vast weight, some sauropods' legs would have been so thick that they would hardly have been able to move.

Scientists debate how high into the trees *Brachiosaurus* could reach. Some say it held its head straight up in the air. However, close study of the neck bones has shown that it probably held its neck at a gentle slope, reaching up to about thirty feet above the ground.

Amounts of food

Jurassic plant food was pretty tough—ferns and fernlike plants. A sauropod had to eat vast amounts to get any nourishment. *Diplodocus* might have had to get through five tons of ferns a day—that's a pile as big as a bus!

Some dinosaur bones had growth rings. Each year, another ring was added, just like the rings on a tree. This suggests that the giant sauropods— and possibly the other dinosaurs— were cold-blooded and could grow only in warm weather.

Modern reptiles, like alligators, are cold-blooded. They are cold when the air is cold, and warm when it is warm. Mammals and birds are warm-blooded and keep their temperature constant.

Diet

Diplodocus was eighty-eight feet long, the longest of the well-known sauropods. This gentle giant must have spent its whole day—and most of the night—munching just to get enough food to survive.

Diplodocus

How many flying *Anurognathus* can you see?

Q: How fast could *Apatosaurus* run?

A: *Apatosaurus* was not a champion sprinter! Some scientists thought the sauropods could gallop, but if they had tried that, their legs would have broken. *Apatosaurus* probably could have managed a slow walk—about six miles per hour at the most.

When the sauropods were first found, in around 1870, some scientists thought they held their legs like lizards, sticking out to the sides. But this could not work, since they would have had to drag their huge stomachs along the ground.

Plodding along

A lot is known about how *Apatosaurus*, from the Late Jurassic of North America, lived. Skeletons and footprints show that it was not a fast mover. It was a close relative of *Diplodocus*, but not as long—only seventy feet from snout to tail tip.

Apatosaurus

Footprints show that *Apatosaurus* walked slowly on land and sometimes into water. It could even swim, prodding a foot into the mud from time to time to help it steer.

zoom in on...

Saltasaurus scales

The titanosaur *Saltasaurus* had large, knoblike bone plates along its back, surrounded by a chain mail of smaller, circular, bony plates. It took a lot of biting to get through this armor.

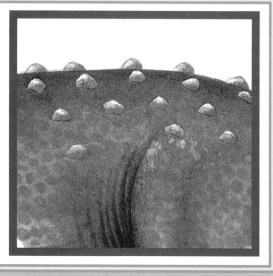

Saltasaurus

Sometimes, sauropods might have reared up if they were under attack. They could then have used their vast weight to crush an attacker, or they could have swiped at them with the long claws on their hands.

Q: Why did sauropods have so few predators?

A: Size has its advantages—most meat eaters think twice about attacking an animal much bigger than they are. They have to balance the benefit of a huge lunch against the risk of being crushed to death. Much easier to attack a smaller beast!

Defense

Sauropods were so huge that they should have been safe from the meat eaters. But by Late Cretaceous times, a group of South American sauropods called the titanosaurs were under attack from giant meat eaters. They even developed armor over their bodies for protection.

Giant plant eaters' world

The giant plant eaters dominated the Late Triassic and Jurassic worlds—prosauropods first, then sauropods throughout the Jurassic. In southern continents, the sauropods continued in force right into the Cretaceous.

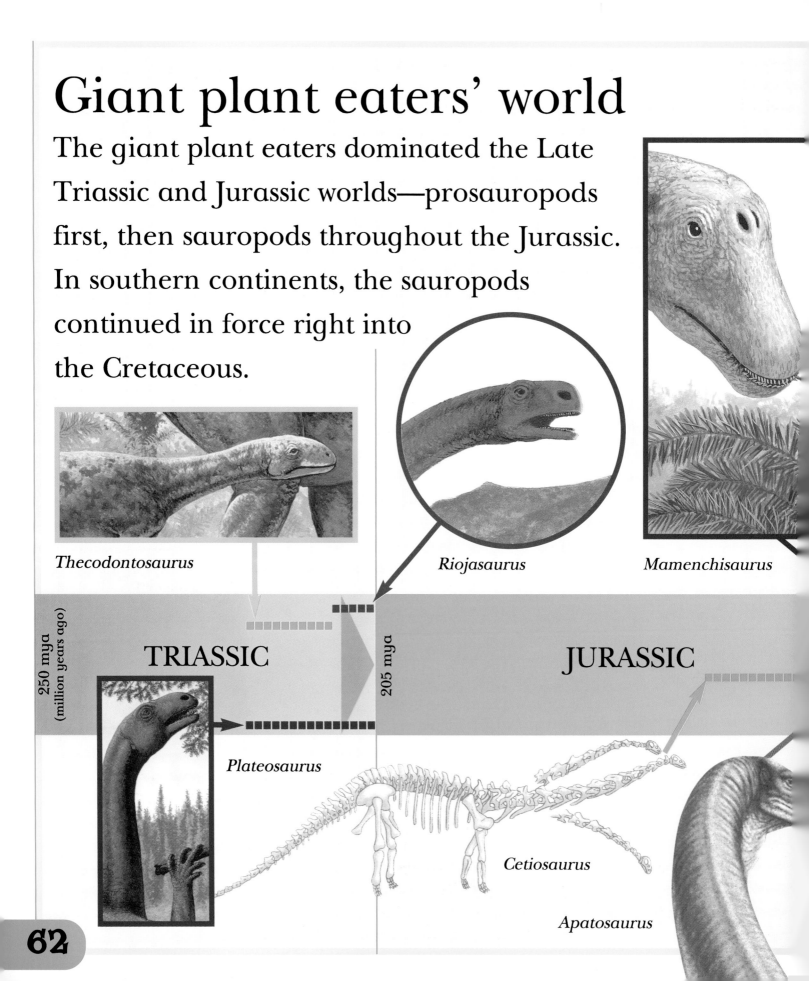

Thecodontosaurus

Riojasaurus

Mamenchisaurus

250 mya
(million years ago)

TRIASSIC

205 mya

JURASSIC

Plateosaurus

Cetiosaurus

Apatosaurus

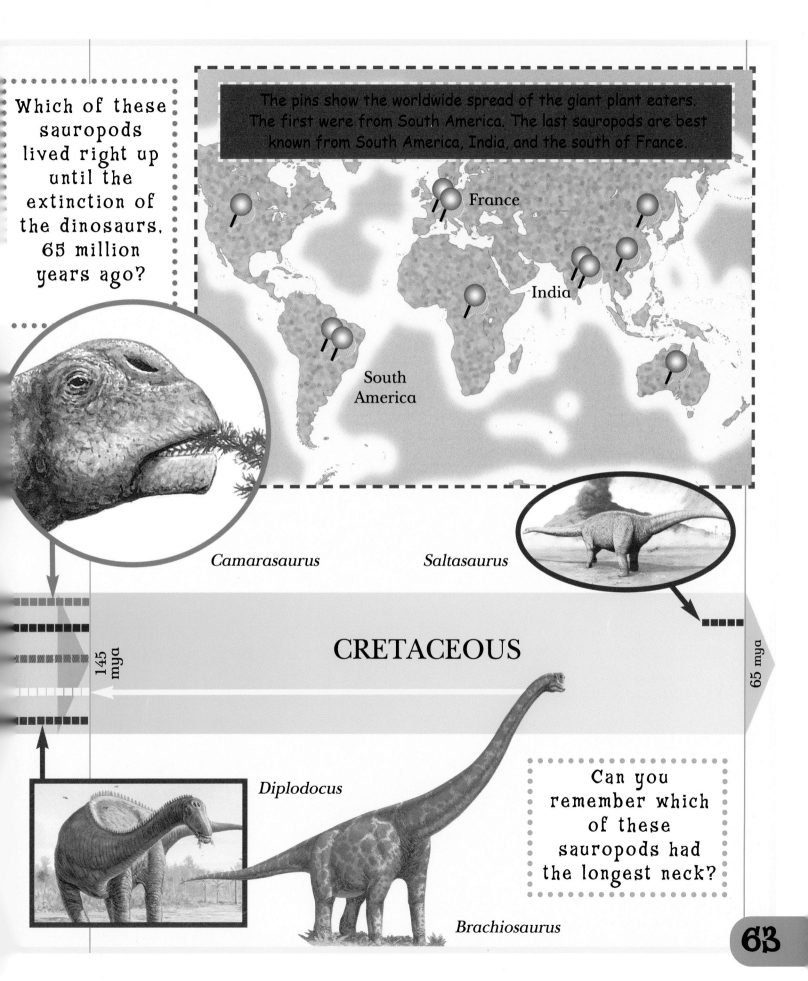

Which of these sauropods lived right up until the extinction of the dinosaurs, 65 million years ago?

The pins show the worldwide spread of the giant plant eaters. The first were from South America. The last sauropods are best known from South America, India, and the south of France.

France

India

South America

Camarasaurus

Saltasaurus

CRETACEOUS

145 mya

65 mya

Diplodocus

Can you remember which of these sauropods had the longest neck?

Brachiosaurus

Chapter 5
Duckbills and boneheads

Duckbills were part of the group called ornithopods. The bonehead group, called marginocephalians, included the boneheads themselves, called pachycephalosaurs, and the horn faces, called ceratopsians.

Stegoceras

Duckbills and boneheads were key dinosaurs of the Cretaceous. In the Late Cretaceous of Canada, herds of the ornithopod *Lambeosaurus* lived alongside the ceratopsian *Styracosaurus* and the smaller pachycephalosaur *Stegoceras*. All the duckbills and boneheads were plant eaters.

Awesome factS
Duckbills and boneheads traveled in huge mixed herds like modern antelope and wildebeest—hundreds of skeletons have been found in some fossil beds.

Lambeosaurus

Styracosaurus

65

Corythosaurus

zoom in on...

Duckbill teeth

Duckbills had hundreds of teeth arranged in tight rows, all designed for chopping tough plants. Some had as many as 2,000 teeth in total.

One of the best-known duckbills, *Corythosaurus* of North America, had a crest shaped like half a plate on its head. It had small hooves on its fingers and toes, suggesting that it walked on all fours. However, *Corythosaurus* also used its hands for grabbing food.

Although hadrosaurs looked like ducks, and may have been able to swim, they spent most of their time running about on dry land. Their huge tails were used for balance. Thin rods of bone called ossified tendons ran along the side of the tail and over the hips. These helped to keep the tail stiff.

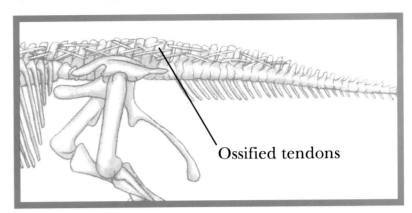

Ossified tendons

What makes a duckbill?

Duckbilled dinosaurs called hadrosaurs were the most successful dinosaurs of all. Hundreds of their skeletons have been found in Late Cretaceous rocks in China, North America, and Mongolia. Hadrosaurs had much the same body, but the heads were very different, often with bizarre crests.

Early ornithopods

The duckbills were common in the Late Cretaceous, but the ornithopod group had been around since the Triassic. The early ones were small and fast-moving, so they could escape from predators.

Lesothosaurus

Lesothosaurus had five fingers on its hand, just like a human. This shows that *Lesothosaurus* was a primitive form, since most later dinosaurs had only three or four fingers. *Lesothosaurus* used its strong little hands to gather leaves, and maybe even to carry them off if they were disturbed.

Q: What did *Lesothosaurus* eat?

A: Like all ornithopods, it ate plants. As it closed its jaws, its teeth rubbed firmly against each other. This shows that it could cut plant stems as if with a large pair of scissors.

Heterodontosaurus

Heterodontosaurus means "different-tooth lizard." It had long canine teeth, rather like a dog. These were not used for piercing flesh, but probably for grasping tough plant stems.

Canine teeth

69

Long-distance journeys

By the Late Jurassic, duckbills and their relatives lived worldwide. One famous one, *Dryosaurus*, was found in North America in 1894. A similar dinosaur was discovered in Tanzania in Africa in 1919. By 1970, it was realized they were identical.

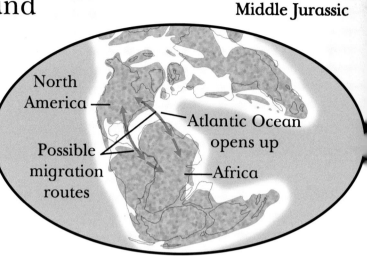

Middle Jurassic

North America

Atlantic Ocean opens up

Possible migration routes

Africa

Identical dinosaurs across the world means long-distance migration. The Atlantic Ocean only began to open in the Middle Jurassic. Before then, *Dryosaurus* could easily have hiked from America to Africa on dry land

Plant eaters often migrated huge distances in search of food. In hot, dry climates, they might have followed the wet seasons north and south to maintain a constant supply of leaves.

How many *Dryosaurus* can you spot?

Dinosaur dung

How do we know what dinosaurs like *Dryosaurus* ate? Fossils of dung, called coprolites, have been found, with chopped up leaves and stalks in them. Like horses, dinosaurs probably couldn't digest it all, so some came out in the dung.

zoom in on...

Dryosaurus had strong arms that it used to reach for leaves. Its jaws were lined with broad teeth, good for chopping up stems. But it had a special feature, seen in all the dinosaurs of the ornithopod group—a horny beak at the front of the jaws, which it used to cut and bite plants.

Dryosaurus

Iguanodon was named by Gideon Mantell in 1825. His wife, Mary Ann, had found some teeth in a pile of rubble beside a road in southern England. He later found more bones in a quarry nearby. The name means "iguana tooth," since Mantell thought its teeth were like those of the modern iguana lizard.

Naming the beast

Many skeletons of the ornithopod *Iguanodon* have been found in Early Cretaceous rocks in southern England, Belgium, France, and Germany. *Iguanodon* had a wicked thumb spike, which it may have used to defend itself.

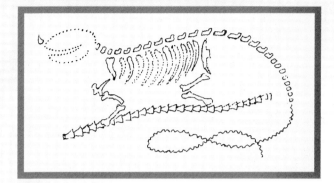

Early collectors only had a few bones of *Iguanodon,* and they thought a heavy, pointed bone was a nose horn (above). Only when whole skeletons were found in 1877 did they see that this bone was in fact the thumb spike.

Iguanodon

Awesome factS

From examination of fossil feet, paleontologists think that *Iguanodon* may have suffered from arthritis in its ankles.

73

How many runners are there?

Runners

Hypsilophodon was a small, fast-moving ornithopod. Great herds of them lived in southern England, and close relatives have been found all over the world. They were among the most successful dinosaur of their day.

Hypsilophodon

Stride length

Length of leg

Dinosaur speeds can be calculated by looking at their leg skeletons and footprints. When an animal runs faster, it takes longer strides—just like you! If you know the stride length, measured from fossil tracks, and the length of the leg, then you can work out the speed.

Q: Did *Hypsilophodon* hide in trees?

A: Some old reconstructions show *Hypsilophodon* perching in a tree. This would have been impossible, however, because its feet would not have been able to grasp a branch. *Hypsilophodon* certainly hid from predators in bushes and found food among the trees, but it was definitely not an oversized perching bird!

Parasaurolophus

Parasaurolophus had one of the most amazing crests—a long tube on top of its head. This was once thought to be a snorkel that allowed the dinosaur to breathe underwater. But there is no hole at the end. It probably allowed one *Parasaurolophus* to identify another.

zoom in on...

Inside the crest

The breathing tubes in a crest ran up from the nostrils to the end of the crest, then back and down to the throat. When a hadrosaur breathed in or out, the air went all around this long set of tubes. This would have made a noise, since the tubes were like part of a trumpet.

Air

Crests and snorkels

The duckbills of the Late Cretaceous, the hadrosaurs, are famous for their amazing headgear—a huge range of crests, horns, and snorkel-like tubes. Scientists have debated what they were for. They may have marked out different species by their various shapes and sounds.

Parasaurolophus

Corythosaurus

Different crests made different noises. Each hadrosaur had its own special honk or toot. In a herd of many different species, hadrosaurs of different types could look and listen for their mates.

Tsintaosaurus

Males and females of a species also had different crest shapes, so they looked and sounded a bit different from each other. One of the *Parasaurolophus* had a shorter crest than the other, but scientists don't know whether the short-crested form was the male or the female.

Parents

Amazing discoveries have been made recently about how duckbills looked after their young. *Maiasaura* of North America cared for their little hatchlings and fed them softened plant fragments. *Maiasaura* means "good mother lizard."

Awesome factS

Maiasaura hatchlings were over three feet long before they left the nest. Until then, their moms brought them tender shoots and leaves to eat.

zoom in on...

Inside a dinosaur egg

Before hatching, a dinosaur baby was very tightly coiled inside the egg. Paleontologists have found some dinosaur eggs that even contain the tiny bones of the embryo, which has died inside.

Embryo ——

Maiasaura mothers dug nests in the ground as big as wading pools. They laid about twenty eggs and stayed around until they hatched. They fed the babies until they were big enough to venture out alone.

Q: Some birds nest in trees, so why didn't dinosaurs?

A: The dinosaur mom would first have had to find a strong tree, then she would have had to climb up somehow. Most dinosaurs were simply too big, or not nimble enough to manage this.

Spot the kidnapper!

The horn faces, called ceratopsians, probably head-butted each other. They may have sized each other up, trying to scare their rival away by looking fierce. They roared and may even have changed the color of the bony frill around their neck. If that didn't work, they might then crash heads and tussle.

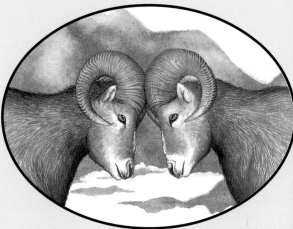

Styracosaurus

Just like boneheads, modern mountain goats crash heads together to see who is strongest in fights for territory or mates.

Pachycephalosaurs arose in the Early Cretaceous, but they are best known from the Late Cretaceous of North America and central Asia. They ran around on two legs, and they were all plant eaters.

Smackers

The boneheads called pachycephalosaurs ("thick-head lizards") are famous for having very thick skull roofs. The males may have had head-butting fights, just like some modern animals.

Domeheads

There were two groups of pachycephalosaurs—one set with very thick, domed skull roofs, the other with lower, flatter skull roofs.

Stegoceras

81

An amazing fossil specimen, found in Mongolia in the 1960s, shows a *Protoceratops* and a *Velociraptor* locked in mortal combat. They were killed by a sandstorm.

How many babies are there?

Protoceratops

Awesome factS

The first Mongolian dinosaurs were named in the 1920s, when expeditions set off into remote northern regions. Now, many amazing dinosaurs are known from there.

Young and old

Skeletons of baby dinosaurs show they were like human babies—big heads, big eyes, short legs, and knobby knees. One of the best series of family fossils found is of the ceratopsian *Protoceratops,* from the Late Cretaceous.

An amazing set of fossil tracks from North America shows how a herd protected its young. The tiny footprints of the babies are in the middle, with the bigger moms' and dads' footprints on the outside.

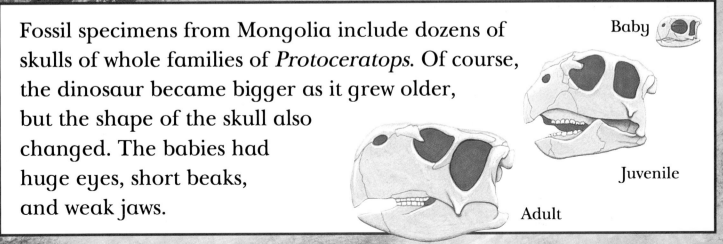

Fossil specimens from Mongolia include dozens of skulls of whole families of *Protoceratops*. Of course, the dinosaur became bigger as it grew older, but the shape of the skull also changed. The babies had huge eyes, short beaks, and weak jaws.

Baby

Juvenile

Adult

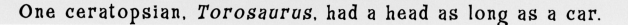

Family protection

Sometimes there is safety in numbers. When a meat eater threatened, many plant eaters could use the herd as a way to protect themselves. Like musk oxen today, ceratopsians may have formed a ring, horned heads outward.

Einosaurus

Albertosaurus

Styracosaurus

Even on their own, the ceratopsians were able to look after themselves. *Albertosaurus* had to be careful when it was faced by the long nose horn and spiky frill of *Styracosaurus*.

Einosaurus babies would stay in the middle of the group when the herd was under attack. The adults would present a united front, with their impressive horns facing the predator.

Ceratopsians had all kinds of face horns, some on the nose, others over the eyes. The neck frill also varied in size and decoration.

Pentaceratops

Chasmosaurus

Triceratops

Q: How fast could a horn face run?

A: Ceratopsians were built to move quite fast. It's likely they could trot, and even get up to twelve miles per hour. They weighed about five tons—the same as a modern elephant. This was much lighter than the sauropods, which could only really walk.

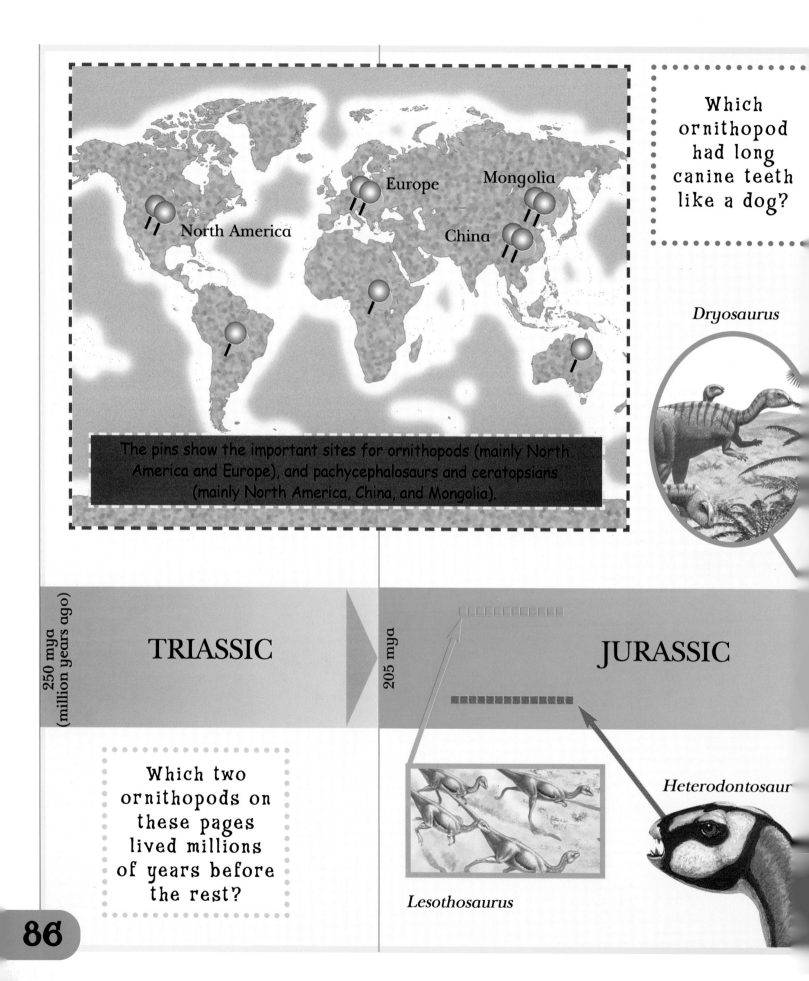

The pins show the important sites for ornithopods (mainly North America and Europe), and pachycephalosaurs and ceratopsians (mainly North America, China, and Mongolia).

Europe

Mongolia

North America

China

Which ornithopod had long canine teeth like a dog?

Dryosaurus

250 mya (million years ago)

TRIASSIC

205 mya

JURASSIC

Which two ornithopods on these pages lived millions of years before the rest?

Heterodontosaur

Lesothosaurus

Duckbill and bonehead world

Ornithopods peaked in the Cretaceous, from *Iguanodon* to the later duckbills. The boneheads (pachycephalosaurs) and horned ceratopsians are only really known from the Late Cretaceous.

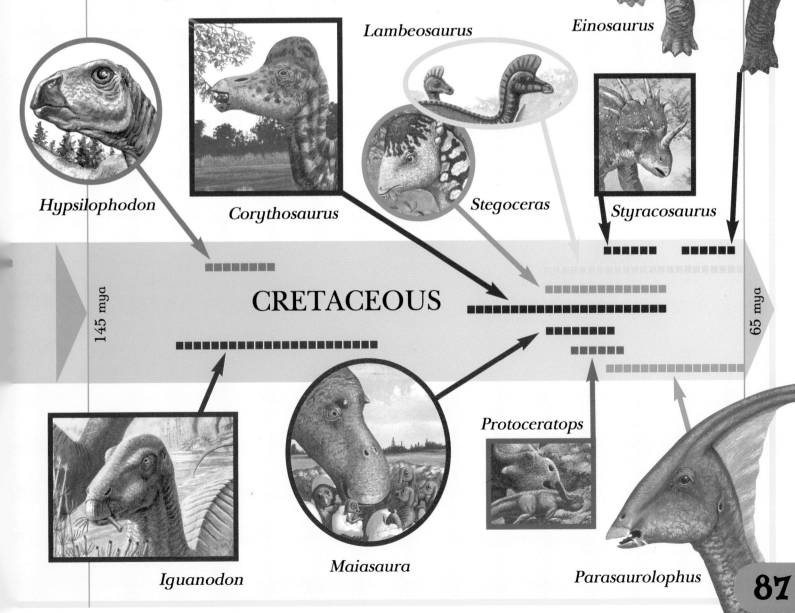

Lambeosaurus

Einosaurus

Hypsilophodon

Corythosaurus

Stegoceras

Styracosaurus

145 mya

CRETACEOUS

65 mya

Protoceratops

Iguanodon

Maiasaura

Parasaurolophus

Chapter 6
Armored dinosaurs

The armored dinosaurs, called the thyreophorans, lived through the Jurassic and Cretaceous. The stegosaurs were particularly important during the Late Jurassic and the ankylosaurs flourished during the Cretaceous.

Ankylosaurs, such as *Hylaeosaurus,* were covered in bony armor and some had large spines along their sides. Stegosaurs, such as *Kentrosaurus,* had spines and plates down the middle of their backs.

Hylaeosaurus

The stegosaurs all had different arrangements of armor plates. *Stegosaurus* from the Late Jurassic of North America had broad plates on its back and tail spikes. *Kentrosaurus* from Tanzania and *Tuojiangosaurus* from China had spines.

Stegosaurus

Tuojiangosaurus

Kentrosaurus

Plates on end

The most famous stegosaur, *Stegosaurus*, had broad, flat plates down its back. People once thought they lay flat to form a kind of shell, but markings at the base of the plates show that they stood upright. What were they for?

zoom in on...

Small brains

Stegosaurus is known as the most stupid dinosaur. It had a brain the size of a walnut. There was actually a second "brain" in the hip region, which operated the hind legs and tail.

Second "brain"

A *Stegosaurus* could trot along at about nine to twelve miles an hour. But stegosaurs were not built for speed. They relied on their plates and spikes for protection.

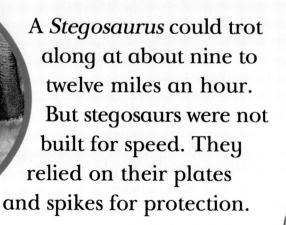

The plates on *Stegosaurus* were for protection and temperature control. Fossils show that they were covered with skin and had large blood vessels. When *Stegosaurus* was angry or hot, it pumped blood over the plates. This made them flush red and also shed heat.

Blood vessels

A recent specimen of *Scelidosaurus*, on display at the Bristol City Museum in England, shows excellent detail of the skull. Some of the skin has even been preserved. The pattern on the skin shows a kind of chain mail of tiny bony plates all over it.

Scelidosaurus was a sleek animal, about thirteen feet long. It trotted around on all fours, seeking ferns and other low plants. Scientists know that it evolved from a two-legged ancestor, since the hind legs are much longer than the front legs. There were seven main rows of bony spines running the length of the body.

Spot two other *Scelidosaurus*.

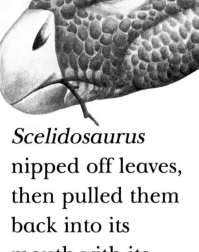

Early trotters

The first armored dinosaur was from the Early Jurassic of southern England. Called *Scelidosaurus*, paleontologists have debated for years whether it is a stegosaur or an ankylosaur—it seems to have been ancestor to both groups.

Scelidosaurus nipped off leaves, then pulled them back into its mouth with its tongue. The cheek pouches saved it from losing bits of food out of the sides.

Scelidosaurus

zoom in on...

Complete skeleton

Scelidosaurus was the first complete dinosaur skeleton and one of the first armored forms ever discovered. It was named in 1860 by Sir Richard Owen.

Monster museum

Many dinosaurs have been found in China since 1970. One of the most spectacular sites is the Dashanpu Quarry at Zigong in Sichuan province, where a group of dinosaurs from the Middle Jurassic has been unearthed. A key discovery was the stegosaur *Tuojiangosaurus*, of which twelve skeletons exist.

Tuojiangosaurus

The Zigong site was discovered by Dong Zhiming, a leading Chinese paleontologist based in Beijing. He has named many amazing new dinosaurs.

Awesome facts
More new species of dinosaur are now being found in China than in any other part of the world.

The Zigong Dinosaur Museum displays skeletons mounted in the usual way, but visitors can also look at some skeletons that are still in the rock. This gives people an idea of what paleontologists see when they first discover fossilized bones.

Kentrosaurus, from the Late Jurassic of Tanzania in Africa, may have been able to rear up and snatch leaves from low levels in trees. The sauropods *Barosaurus* and *Brachiosaurus* fed at higher levels.

Kentrosaurus

zoom in on...

Stegosaur teeth

Stegosaurs had long, narrow jaws and teeth that were quite short. The jaws were not built for chomping twigs and tough plant food, nor were the teeth—the teeth had a shaped edge that was very useful for cutting leaves.

Leaf eaters

Stegosaurs were plant eaters. They fed on low bushes and trees, tearing out leaves and chomping them. However, they mostly ate soft leaves, since their teeth were not very powerful.

Stegosaurs probably ate ferns and seed ferns close to the ground, and the lower leaves of conifer trees, such as the monkey puzzle. There were no deciduous trees or flowering plants in the Late Jurassic.

Gasosaurus

Squaring up

It seems certain that armored dinosaurs used their armor to stand up to predators. *Huayangosaurus*, a stegosaur from the Middle Jurassic of China, could face up to the meat eater *Gasosaurus* just by looking scary.

Stegosaurs might have used their sharp spines to square up to rivals as well. The bigger one probably scared the smaller one away.

Q: What could a stegosaur do with its tail?

A: Whack its enemies! There were powerful muscles in the tail, and it could deliver a wounding blow. A meat eater could get a slash up to three feet long in its flesh. No thanks!

Stegosaurs were mo placid animals, b attacker would defense—red and plates spiked, sw

zoom in on...

Thick legs

Ankylosaurs had short, fat legs with unusually broad and short bones. The bones had to be stout to support the great weight of all the armor.

Hylaeosaurus

...us and *Hylaeosaurus*
...ed herds in the Early
...southern England.
...aurs were very
...t they had
...n their armor.

Walking works

The ankylosaurs were slow movers and were smaller than the stegosaurs. They didn't have to move fast—with a heavy armor of plates all over their body, they were safe from attackers. Even if it wanted to, an ankylosaur couldn't shift all that weight at any faster than a stroll.

Polacanthus

Fossilized tracks show that ankylosaurs moved slowly. The footprints are spaced close together, suggesting that the maximum speed they could reach was perhaps six miles per hour—the same speed you go when you jog. You could easily beat one in a sprint race!

Flower chompers

The ankylosaurs lived mainly in lowland areas near lakes and rivers. They fed on lush plants around these watery habitats, but could not reach up high into trees or go up on their hind legs.

How many different kinds of flowers?

Q: Why did some ankylosaurs have broader mouths than others?

A: The shape of their mouths tells us about the food they ate. A broad mouth, like *Sauropelta*'s, means it cropped all kinds of plants and flowers. A narrow mouth, like *Polacanthus*'s, means it probably only ate certain plants.

Polacanthus

During the Cretaceous, there were big changes in plant life. The earliest ankylosaurs fed on ferns, seed ferns, and low conifers, but the group really took off after the flowering plants appeared in the Mid Cretaceous. The ankylosaurs would have especially liked the new plants—early roses, vines, and magnolias.

Sauropelta

Sauropelta, from the Mid Cretaceous of North America, lived side by side with the meat eater *Deinonychus*. But the ankylosaur ignored the slashing attacks of the predator—if *Deinonychus* tried any nonsense, it would just break its claws on *Sauropelta's* armored back.

Baby snatchers

One of the scariest ankylosaurs was *Edmontonia*. Powerful and sturdy, this ankylosaur also sprouted great spines along its sides. It was about twenty feet long, and weighed up to eleven tons. Attackers would think twice before tackling such a monster!

A baby *Edmontonia* may have seemed a tasty meal for a meat eater, but th parents would soo scare it off.

Edmontonia

Awesome facts

Two specimens of *Edmontonia* were mummified—dried out by the heat—and they show how the spikes were arranged.

Viewed head-on, *Edmontonia* was an amazing sight, with a tiny armor-plated head and a massive body with forward-pointing spines. Its main enemy, *Albertosaurus*, would know to keep clear.

Albertosaurus

zoom in on...

Tank features

Ankylosaurs look at first like turtles, but they were much, much bigger. *Edmontonia* was one of the biggest, and was built like an army tank. It couldn't move very fast, but with its great weight, powerful legs, and fearsome armor, it must have been unstoppable.

Ankylosaurs had a special pattern of armor plates over their heads. There was a second layer of bones over the normal skull bones. The armor plating even extended to special bony ridges over the nostrils and a bony eyelid cover. No predator could possibly bite through all that!

Boned up

Ankylosaurs were the best protected animals of all time. Even the head had its own special armor plating. *Talarurus*, of the Late Cretaceous of Mongolia, is a typical ankylosaur. It was protected from its predators by armor, bony spines, and a bony ball on the end of its tail.

How many *Talarurus* can you spot?

Talarurus

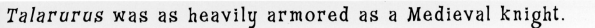
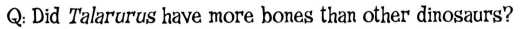

Q: Did *Talarurus* have more bones than other dinosaurs?

A: A typical dinosaur had about 350 bones in its skull and skeleton. Ankylosaurs like *Talarurus* had far more—their armor could add about three hundred major bony plates and spines along the back, plus fifty or so extra bone plates around the head, and hundreds of small bone plates in the skin. Humans have only about 250 bones.

Awesome facts
Ankylosaurs had so much armor that the skeleton and armor together could make up more than half their total body weight.

Fighting

Ankylosaur armor was for defense, but also for fighting. Male ankylosaurs probably fought their predators and each other. Unlike *Hylaeosaurus* and *Sauropelta,* with their straight tails, *Talarurus* and *Euoplocephalus* had bony tail clubs to fight with.

zoom in on...

Bony tail

The tail club was made from the last three or four vertebrae in the tail, fused into a hard, bony blob. It was heavy and could very easily knock out a predator.

Euoplocephalus

Male ankylosaurs probably fought rivals by posing and roaring. The smaller one would eventually be scared off. If the two were equally matched, they might barge into each other, whacking with their tails. But the armor would protect them from serious injury.

Carnotaurus

The tail club was like a steel wrecking ball used to demolish walls. Ankylosaurs could kill predators with their tail clubs if they hit them hard enough in the right place.

Euoplocephalus from the Late Cretaceous of North America lived at the same time as the meat eater *Carnotaurus*. They must have faced each other often, but after it had been whacked about a bit, *Carnotaurus* would probably have learned not to tackle the ankylosaur.

Euoplocephalus

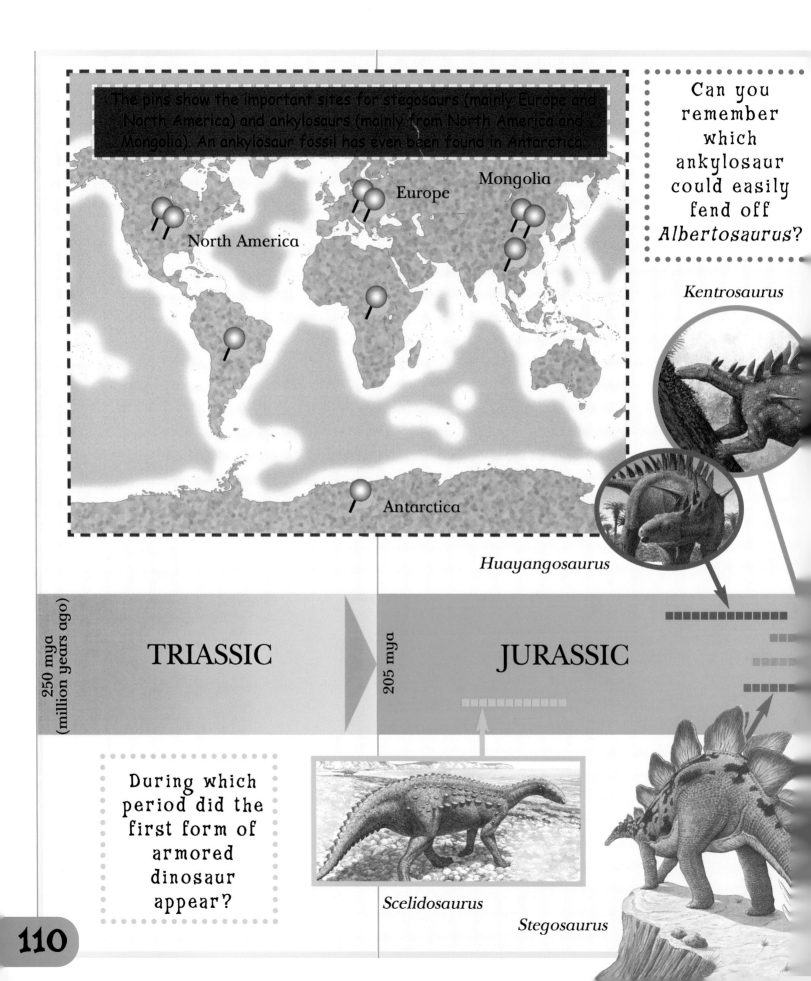

The pins show the important sites for stegosaurs (mainly Europe and North America) and ankylosaurs (mainly from North America and Mongolia). An ankylosaur fossil has even been found in Antarctica.

Mongolia

Europe

North America

Antarctica

Can you remember which ankylosaur could easily fend off *Albertosaurus*?

Kentrosaurus

Huayangosaurus

250 mya (million years ago)

TRIASSIC

205 mya

JURASSIC

During which period did the first form of armored dinosaur appear?

Scelidosaurus

Stegosaurus

Armored dinosaur world

The armored dinosaurs split into two groups in the Middle Jurassic—the plated stegosaurs and the bone-covered ankylosaurs. Stegosaurs were important in the Late Jurassic, ankylosaurs in the Late Cretaceous.

Edmontonia

Hylaeosaurus

Euoplocephalus

Talarurus

145 mya

CRETACEOUS

65 mya

Polacanthus

Tuojiangosaurus

Sauropelta

Chapter 7
Alongside the dinosaurs

Dinosaurs were not the only animals alive
in the Mesozoic era. Many smaller creatures
lived around ponds and in the undergrowth—
frogs, turtles, lizards, crocodiles, and mammals.
By the Cretaceous, snakes and birds had
also appeared.

During the Mid Cretaceous, many
of the huge dinosaurs could walk
past a whole scene of modern-looking
animals, hardly knowing they
were there. All kinds of fish
swam in ponds, and insects
crawled and flew around.

Spot three beetles.

113

Q: **What did plesiosaurs eat?**

A: Plesiosaurs ate fish, ammonites, nautiloids, and belemnites. Belemnites, like nautiloids, were ancient, squidlike creatures, with a bulletlike internal skeleton. Ammonites were coiled shellfish, which were also related to modern squids.

Nautiloid

Ammonite

Liopleurodon

Mososaurus

The pliosaurs, such as *Liopleurodon*, had massive skulls. They fed on other marine reptiles, like smaller plesiosaurs and ichthyosaurs. The lizardlike *Mososaurus* was one of the last sea reptiles. It also fed on other marine reptiles, as well as ammonites and fish

Plesiosaurs

The plesiosaurs were a successful group of marine reptiles that lived throughout the Mesozoic era. There were two kinds— the long-necked plesiosaurs and the short-necked, massive pliosaurs. But these were not dinosaurs.

Elasmosaurus

Plesiosaurs, such as *Elasmosaurus*, propelled themselves by a kind of underwater flying (above). They moved their strong fins back and down, then turned them and brought them up and forward in a great curved loop.

115

Ichthyosaurs

Ichthyosaurs were amazing marine reptiles. They were completely adapted to life at sea, with streamlined bodies, powerful tail fins, and long snouts. They lived through the Triassic and Jurassic periods, but died out before the end of the Cretaceous.

Although they look like fish, ichthyosaurs were reptiles and had to breathe air. They probably came to the surface every few minutes for a gulp of air.

Ichthyosaurs could not come out on land to lay eggs, so they gave birth at sea. Some amazing fossils show the mother ichthyosaur in the process of giving birth to live young, just like a dolphin.

Awesome facts

There are some astonishing fossils of mother ichthyosaurs with as many as ten unborn babies inside the body.

Ichthyosaurs probably swam around in large groups, or schools, just like modern dolphins. This would help to protect them from predators from the sky. They might also have hunted fish as a pack.

Rhamphorhynchus

Ichthyosaur

Where's the baby?

Many beautiful and complete skeletons of Jurassic ichthyosaurs have been found. The ichthyosaurs that fell to the bottom of the sea into black mud that had no oxygen in it were especially well preserved. No oxygen meant no scavengers, so the skeletons remained undamaged when they were buried.

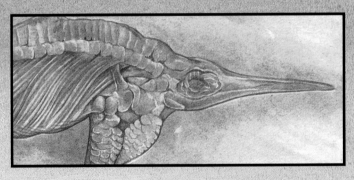

Quetzalcoatlus

Pterosaurs

Pterosaurs, or "winged lizards," were a common sight in the Mesozoic era, soaring high over the heads of the dinosaurs. Like marine reptiles, pterosaurs were not dinosaurs, but they were quite closely related.

Pterodaustro

Pteranodon

Many pterosaurs ate insects, but the larger ones all seem to have been fish eaters. Some of them skimmed over the waves and scooped fish out. Others dive-bombed into the water, snapping at unsuspecting fish.

118

Dimorphodon

Rhamphorhynchus

Baby pterosaurs hatched from eggs that were laid in nests, probably on cliff tops. The parents brought back fish and other morsels for them. It probably took some time before the babies were big and strong enough to fly by themselves.

Peranodon

zoom in on...

Wingspan

Pterosaurs ranged in size from tiny ones to real giants. _Quetzalcoatlus_ had a wingspan of forty feet or more— much bigger than any modern bird.

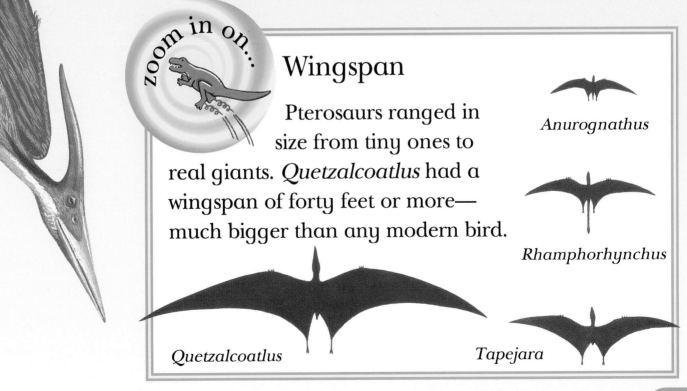

Anurognathus

Rhamphorhynchus

Quetzalcoatlus

Tapejara

119

Archaeopteryx

Several fossilized feathers have been found, which show every detail of the structure of the feather, but not its color. There are now seven fossils of *Archaeopteryx*, all showing the feathers in place. This is how we know that it had wings just like a modern bird.

120

Awesome factS

If the *Archaeopteryx* fossils had not had their feathers preserved, they would have been identified as raptor dinosaurs.

Birds

Cretaceous skies were full of birds as well as pterosaurs. *Archaeopteryx*, the first bird, lived in the Late Jurassic of Germany. More and more bird groups appeared during the Cretaceous, but most of the modern bird groups came later.

Modern birds have short, bony parts to their tail, no teeth, and no hand claws. *Archaeopteryx* is the perfect "missing link" between modern birds and the dinosaurs. It had feathers and wings, but it also had a long, bony tail, teeth in its jaws, and hands on its wings.

121

Chapter 8
Where did they go?

The world of the dinosaurs came to an end, quite suddenly, 65 million years ago (mya). Scientists are still debating what happened. How could such an amazing group of beasts as the dinosaurs suddenly become extinct?

Q: Did mammals eat all the dinosaurs' eggs?

A: One theory for the extinction was that mammals ate all the dinosaurs' eggs. But the mammals had been around all through the age of the dinosaurs, and they hadn't done it before.

The mammals did not die out—obviously! They were small and could survive changes in climate better than the dinosaurs.

There were huge volcanic eruptions in India 65 mya that pumped out lava and produced huge dust clouds. These blew all around the earth and would have blacked out the sun, leading to darkness and cold.

Whatever happened 5 mya, the whole natural ystem collapsed. If the lant eaters died out first, then the redators would have gone too, since ney would have had nothing to eat.

Impact!

There is now very strong evidence that Earth was hit by a huge meteorite, about six miles across, 65 million years ago. The impact threw up huge clouds of dust, blacking out the sun, and leading to freezing, dark conditions for a year or more.

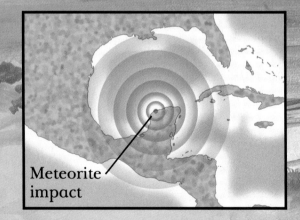

Meteorite impact

The meteorite hit Earth on the coast of Mexico. A huge crater, 124 miles across, has been found, buried beneath younger rocks. The crater was mainly in the sea 65 million years ago.

When a big meteorite hits Earth, it has enormous impact. It drives a long way into the ground and then turns to vapor. Then, very quickly, there is a huge back blast and millions of tons of rock and dust are thrown back up into the air.

The force of the back blast forms a huge crater.

Meteorite drives into Earth

Back blast makes crater

After the dust cloud came a huge fireball of burning gases. Enormous wildfires swept over much of the planet, burning everything in their way.

Chapter 9
Rise of the mammals

Mammals were around through the whole age of the dinosaurs, but they were mostly small animals, about the size of a rat. The dinosaurs probably didn't even see them. The mammals kept out of the way and hunted mainly at night.

The first mammals hunted insects and other small creatures while the dinosaurs slept. They could not grow large because the dinosaurs were so successful that nothing could compete with them.

Q: What is a mammal?

A: Mammals have hair and they are warm-blooded. They also feed their young on milk and look after them. They have larger brains than reptiles. Modern mammals include mice, cats, elephants, whales—and humans.

How many
mammals can
you see?

Early mammals

After the dinosaurs disappeared 65 million years ago, Earth was a strange, empty place. Some birds flew among the trees and small mammals scuttled in and out of the undergrowth. No one then could have predicted that these mammals would rise to rule the world.

Awesome facts

All modern mammals, from tiny bats to huge whales, first appeared within 10 million years after the dinosaurs had gone.

Warm blood

zoom in on...

All mammals are warm-blooded. They can control their body temperatures. This means they can hunt at night and live in cold places, like the modern polar bear. Reptiles and fish are cold-blooded, which means they are always as hot, or as cold, as the air or water around them.

Early mammals in North America included some catlike and monkeylike creatures, and even some gliders. But none of them was bigger than a dog.

129

Competition

By 50 million years ago, many kinds of mammals had evolved. Some modern groups had appeared, like horses and whales, but mammals did not have it all their own way. Terror-birds ruled the world!

Q: Where did whales come from?

A: Whales breathe air and feed their young milk, so, although they live in the sea like fish, they are mammals. The first whales lived over 50 million years ago, and they were like seals. They evolved from big, meat-eating land animals like *Mesonyx*.

Mesonyx   Blue whale

Monkeys, apes, and humans are called primates. The first primates looked like squirrels, but they had big brains and long tails for balancing as they ate fruit and leaves in the trees.

The top predators 50 million years ago were not mammals, but giant birds. At about ten feet tall, *Diatryma* was a fearsome hunter and fed on smaller mammals, including the ancestors of modern horses. These early horses were only about the size of a terrier dog and the bird crushed them in its powerful jaws. *Diatryma*'s head was about the size of that of a modern horse.

Diatryma

Mammal evolution

About 20 million years ago there were huge changes in landscapes worldwide. Grass had evolved and huge grasslands spread over the continents. Mammals had to adapt, and grass eaters became very important.

Early elephants had tusks on top of their mouths (like they do today), below their mouths, or sometimes both above and below.

Paraceratherium was a giant rhinoceros with a long neck and no horn. At about twenty feet tall, this grass eater was the biggest land mammal of all time.

132

Q: What did early horses look like?

A: Horses have always looked like horses, but early horses were very small and they had four toes. Over time, horses became bigger and lost their side toes. So now they have a single toe, known as a hoof.

Modern horse

Early horse

Giant armadillos called glyptodonts were early South American mammals. They had body armor and even a spiky tail club. They looked like ankylosaurs, but were not related.

Chapter 10
Dinosaurs today

Although the dinosaurs themselves all died out 65 million years ago, there are still a lot of their relatives around today, as reptiles and birds. Modern reptiles are a mixed bunch—they do not rule the world as they did in the age of the dinosaurs, but there are still 6,500 species of them around the world.

Lizards are the biggest group of living reptiles, with 3,700 species. Many are small and live in hot countries. Most feed on insects, but a few eat plants. The marine iguana (left) is unusual —it dives in the sea for tiny marine creatures.

Turtles and tortoises live both on land and in the sea. They all have a shell that provides excellent protection from attack. Tortoises on land move about slowly, looking for plants or insects to eat. Marine turtles are big—some are six feet long. They live at sea, but have to lay their eggs on land.

zoom in on...

Living fossils

One unusual reptile, the tuatara of New Zealand, is sometimes called a living fossil because it seems to have survived from the age of the dinosaurs. The tuatara looks just like its earliest ancestors from the Late Triassic period, 220 million years ago.

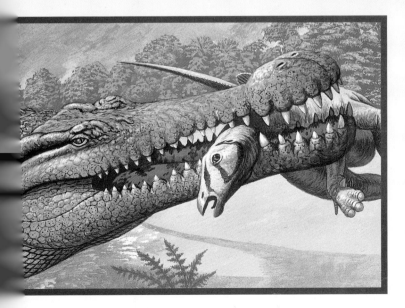

Crocodiles are the closest reptile relatives of dinosaurs. Today's crocodiles mainly hunt underwater, by sneaking up on animals at the water's edge, then grabbing them. Crocodiles that lived with the dinosaurs (left) could be huge, and some ate dinosaurs.

135

Living on

Birds are the closest thing to living dinosaurs. They may not look much like them, but it is now clear that birds arose from small meat eaters. The first bird, *Archaeopteryx* (see page 120), had a dinosaur skeleton and bird wings and feathers.

A clue to the ancestry of birds can be seen in modern hoatzin chicks. Hoatzins live along river banks in South America. The chicks have claws on their wings, just like *Archaeopteryx*.

zoom in on...

Bird teeth

Birds today do not have teeth. But they can still produce teeth in laboratory experiments. This shows that, deep in their heritage, they once had teeth but lost them over time.

Modern birds come in all shapes and sizes, from tiny hummingbirds, no bigger than a moth, to the giant albatross and condor. Birds live all over the world, from penguins at the poles to parrots in the tropics.

An ostrich looks very much like the ostrich dinosaur, *Struthiomimus*, but they are not closely related. Ostrich ancestors could fly, then they lost that ability. Ostriches still have small wings, but they are now only used for keeping cool. Ostriches can run very fast to catch their prey, so they don't need to be able to fly.

Q: Do we know everything about dinosaurs?

A: No! Scientists learn new things about dinosaurs every day. Each year, about twenty new species are named, and there are lots more to be found. New studies tell us new things about how dinosaurs lived, and powerful computers allow paleontologists to calculate exactly how dinosaurs walked and ran. All this means that more and more accurate dinosaur models can be made. Life as a dinosaur paleontologist is never dull!

truthiomimus

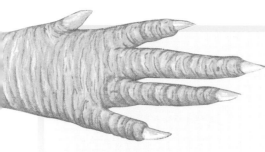

Glossary

Amber

Fossilized resin from a conifer tree.

Ammonite

A prehistoric shellfish with a coiled shell, common in Mesozoic seas.

Amphibian

A backboned animal that lives both in water and on land, such as a frog.

Ancestor

A historical forerunner of an animal group.

Ankylosaur

An armored plant-eating dinosaur, with a covering of bony plates and sometimes a bony knob on the end of its tail.

Belemnite

A prehistoric shellfish with a straight, bullet-shaped internal shell, like a modern cuttlefish.

Ceratopsian

A plant-eating dinosaur with a bony frill at the back of its neck and one or more horns on its face.

Cold-blooded

A cold-blooded animal needs to take its body heat from outside sources, sometimes by basking in the sun.

Conifer

An evergreen tree, such as a pine, with cones and needles.

Continental drift

The movement of the continents over time.

Coprolite

A fossilized poop.

Cretaceous

The geological period that lasted from 145 to 65 million years ago.

Cynodont

A mammal-like reptile similar to the very first mammals.

Deciduous tree

A tree that sheds its leaves.

DNA

Stands for *Deoxyribonucleic acid*, a chemical inside every plant and animal cell, which carries the information that controls the development of the body. All species have different DNA.

Duckbill

An ornithopod dinosaur of the Late Cretaceous, with a ducklike snout. Duckbills are sometimes called hadrosaur

Evolution

The processes by which all plants and animals appeare billions of years ago, and how they changed over tim

Fossil

The remains of any ancient plant or animal, usually preserved in rock.

Gene

A specific part of the DNA chemical, which carries the code for a particular feature of a plant or animal.

Geological

Anything to do with the study of rocks.

Hadrosaur

An ornithopod dinosaur of the Late Cretaceous, with a ducklike snout. Hadrosaurs are sometimes called duckbills.

Hatchling

A young animal that has just hatched out of the egg.

Ichthyosaur

A sea reptile common in the Mesozoic, which had a streamlined body and swimming paddles.

Jurassic

The geological period that lasted from 205 to 145 million years ago.

Juvenile

A young animal, older than a baby, but younger than an adult.

Keratin

The protein that makes up reptile scales, as well as birds' feathers and human hair and nails.

Limestone

Rock made from lime (calcium carbonate), often created by the shells of ancient animals.

Mammal

A backboned animal with hair, which feeds its young on milk, such as a cat, a horse, or a human.

Marginocephalian

A plant-eating dinosaur with armored margins (borders) on the back of its skull, such as a ceratopsian or a pachycephalosaur.

Mesozoic

The geological era that lasted from 250 to 65 million years ago, sometimes known as the "age of dinosaurs."

Meteorite

A lump of rock from space that hits Earth or any other planet.

Migration

The movement of animals from one place to another in search of food or breeding grounds.

Nautiloid

A long and pointed prehistoric shellfish.

139

Ornithischian

A "bird-hipped" dinosaur, such as an ornithopod, marginocephalian, or thyreophoran.

Ornithopod

A two-legged plant eater from the ornithischian group, such as *Iguanodon* and the duckbills.

Ossified tendon

A muscular attachment that has turned to bone and acts as a strengthening rod.

Pachycephalosaur

A plant-eating dinosaur with a hugely thickened skull roof.

Paleontologist

A person who studies fossils.

Pangaea

An ancient supercontinent that consisted of all the modern continents joined together as one.

Plesiosaur

A long-necked Mesozoic sea reptile that hunted fish.

Pliosaur

A short-necked Mesozoic sea reptile that hunted other smaller sea reptiles—a relative of the plesiosaurs.

Predator

A meat eater—an animal that hunts others for food.

Prehistoric

"Before history"—describes anything from ancient times, such as the dinosaurs.

Prosauropod

A plant-eating dinosaur with a long neck and tail, from the Late Triassic or Early Jurassic periods.

Pterosaur

A flying reptile of the Mesozoic, closely related to the dinosaurs.

Radioactivity

"Rays" of chemical energy that are given off at fixed rates. Measuring radioactive elements in ancient rocks allows geologists to calculate the ages of the rocks.

Raptor

A hunter—often refers to dinosaurs like *Deinonychus* and *Velociraptor*.

Reptile

A backboned animal with scales that lives on land and lays eggs, such as a dinosaur, a crocodile, or a lizard. Ichthyosaurs and plesiosaurs were marine reptiles.

Sandstone

Rock made from grains of sand cemented together.

Saurischian

A "lizard-hipped" dinosaur, such as a theropod or a sauropodomorph.

Sauropod

A long-necked, long-tailed, giant plant-eating dinosaur.

Sauropodomorph

The group name for large, long-necked, plant-eating dinosaurs, such as sauropods and prosauropods.

Scavenger

A meat eater that feeds off animals that have died or have been killed by others.

Skeleton

The framework of bones inside the body of a backboned animal.

Species

One particular kind of plant or animal, such as *Tyrannosaurus rex*, the panda, or human beings.

Stegosaur

A plant-eating dinosaur with bony plates and spines sticking upright along its back and tail.

Supercontinent

"Big continent," such as Pangaea, which is made up of several continents.

Theropod

A meat-eating dinosaur.

Thyreophoran

An armored dinosaur, such as a stegosaur or an ankylosaur.

Triassic

The geological period that lasted from 250 to 205 million years ago.

Vertebra (plural **Vertebrae**)

An element of the backbone. Each vertebra is like a cotton spool with bits sticking out for the ribs and muscles. Together, the vertebrae make up the backbone.

Warm-blooded

A warm-blooded animal, such as a mammal or a bird, creates heat inside its body from the food it eats.

Index